Venezuela ABCs

A Book About the People and Places of Venezuela

by Sharon Katz Cooper   illustrated by Stacey Previn

Special thanks to our advisers for their expertise:

Luis Palacios, Mason Fellow
Harvard University

Susan Kesselring, M.A., Literacy Educator
Rosemount–Apple Valley–Eagan (Minnesota) School District

Editor: Jill Kalz
Designers: Joe Anderson and Abbey Fitzgerald
Page Production: Melissa Kes
Art Director: Nathan Gassman
Associate Managing Editor: Christianne Jones
The illustrations in this book were created with acrylics.

Picture Window Books
5115 Excelsior Boulevard
Suite 232
Minneapolis, MN 55416
877-845-8392
www.picturewindowbooks.com

Printed in the United States of America.

Library of Congress Cataloging-in-Publication Data
Cooper, Sharon Katz.
Venezuela ABCs : a book about the people and places of Venezuela /
by Sharon Katz Cooper ; illustrated by Stacey Previn.
p. cm. — (Country ABCs)
Includes bibliographical references and index.
ISBN-13: 978-1-4048-2250-4 (library binding)
ISBN-10: 1-4048-2250-X (library binding)
1. Venezuela—Juvenile literature. 2. Alphabet books. I. Previn,
Stacey. II. Title.
F2308.5.C67 2006
972.85—dc22   2006027233

Hola! (OH-lah)

That means "Hi!" in Spanish, Venezuela's official language. Venezuela is a South American country near the equator. It's known for its mountains, plains, and many natural resources. Neighboring countries include Colombia, Brazil, and Guyana.

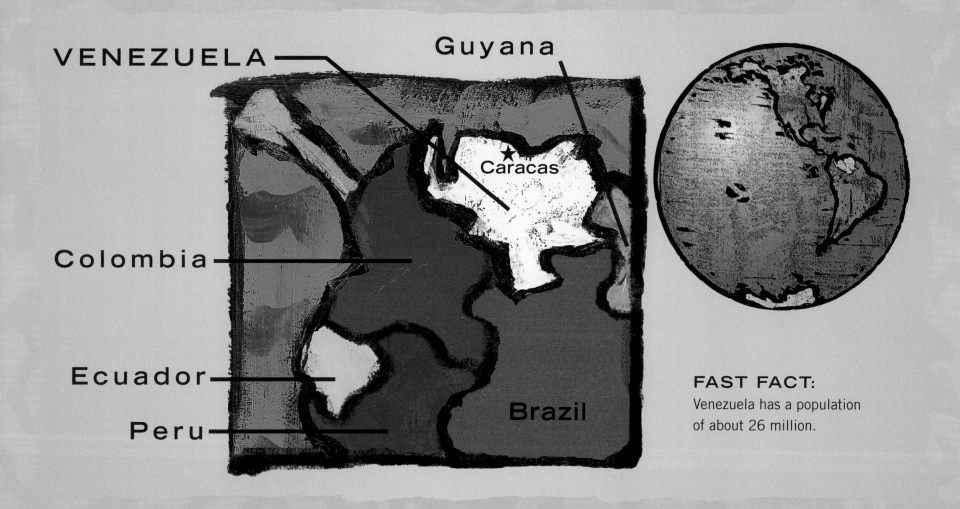

VENEZUELA

Guyana

Caracas

Colombia

Ecuador

Peru

Brazil

FAST FACT:
Venezuela has a population of about 26 million.

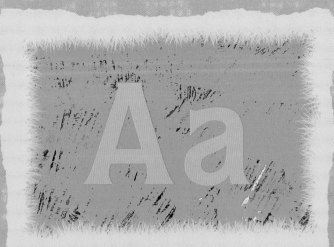

A is for art.

Art has always played an important part in the lives of the Venezuelan people. Early Venezuelan artists painted religious pictures and historical events. Today, the country's artists are best known for their kinetic art style. This art style represents the energy and strong spirit of the Venezuelan people.

FAST FACT:
Kinetic art uses light and color to create the effect of movement.

B is for Simón Bolívar.

Simón Bolívar is a Venezuelan hero. He led the fight to free Venezuela from Spain during the Venezuelan War of Independence (1811–1812). Today, the country's unit of money is called the bolivar, in honor of the hero. Bolivar is also the name of Venezuela's tallest mountain and one of the country's 23 states.

FAST FACT:
Almost every town square in Venezuela has a statue of Simón Bolívar riding a white horse.

C is for Caracas.

Caracas is Venezuela's capital city. It is a busy, modern city of more than 5 million people. The National Capitol building sits in the center of Caracas. It is so large that it takes up an entire city block.

FAST FACT:
Caracas' nickname is *La Sucursal del Cielo*, which means "Branch of Heaven."

D is for dolphins.

Several different kinds of dolphins play in the seas around Venezuela. Visitors to Margarita Island, an island off the coast of Venezuela, can watch these friendly sea mammals swimming around their boats.

FAST FACT:
Crocodiles, snakes, and freshwater manatees live in and around the rivers of Venezuela.

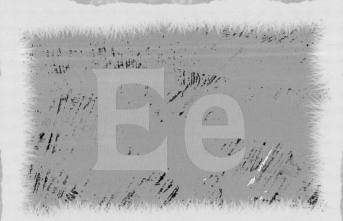

E is for El Dorado.

One of the most famous stories in Venezuela and its surrounding countries is the legend of El Dorado. The story says that an Indian chief paddled a raft to the middle of a lagoon each year and dumped gold into the water. Many explorers searched for the gold, but no one ever found it.

FAST FACT:
Today, Venezuela's oil is often called "black gold" because it produces so much money for the country.

F is for flag.

Venezuela's flag has the coat of arms in the upper left corner, eight stars in the middle, and three stripes: one yellow, one blue, and one red. Yellow stands for the richness of the earth. Blue is for the Atlantic Ocean nearby. The stars stand for the eight provinces that fought for Venezuela's independence in the early 1800s. Red stands for the blood that was spilled to win Venezuela's freedom from Spanish rule.

G is for Rómulo Gallegos.

Rómulo Gallegos was a famous Venezuelan writer. He wrote several novels. His most famous is *Doña Bárbara*, a story about the struggle between tradition and progress. Gallegos was also involved in public service. During his career, he was a member of congress, the mayor of Caracas, and the president of Venezuela in 1948.

H is for hallaca
(eye-YAH-kah).

Hallaca is a favorite food in Venezuela.

To make it, cooks wrap banana leaves and

corn flour pancakes around spicy beef,

pork, chicken, olives, and vegetables.

Then the wraps are steamed.

FAST FACT:
Venezuelans eat *hallacas* as a treat
at Christmastime.

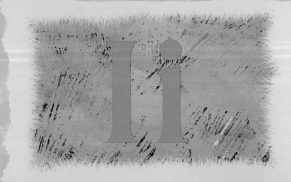

I is for iguana.

Green iguanas are common throughout Venezuela. These medium-sized reptiles like to live near water and forests and spend a lot of time in trees. They eat leaves and small flowers.

FAST FACT:
Other reptiles in Venezuela include the caiman and the largest snake in the world: the anaconda.

J is for joropo
(hoh-ROH-poh).

Joropo is the national music of Venezuela. It was first played long ago on the country's central plains. Musicians play *joropo* with harps, maracas, and guitar-like instruments. The music is fast and lively.

K is for kilograms.

Venezuelans use the metric system to measure things. Kilograms and grams are common measures of weight. Kilometers, meters, and centimeters are common measures of distance. Venezuelans measure temperature in degrees Celsius.

FAST FACT:
A kilogram is equal to 2.2 pounds.

Ll

L is for llanos.

The llanos are the flat central plains of Venezuela. They are located east of the country's big mountain ranges. During the dry season, the plains dry up, and people are able to travel across them by horseback. During the rainy season, however, the llanos flood, and people must use canoes to get from place to place.

FAST FACT:
Venezuelan cowboys are called *llaneros* (yah-NAYR-ohs). They wear wide-brimmed hats called sombreros to protect them from the sun.

M is for mango.

Mangoes are sweet, colorful fruits that are green, yellow, and red on the outside and orange on the inside. They grow in large numbers in Venezuelan rain forests. Venezuelans usually buy mangoes in outdoor fruit markets.

FAST FACT:
Venezuelans love to eat grilled foods. They grill beef and fish and eat the meat with fruits, rice, salad, and bread.

N is for niña
(NEE-nha).

Niña is the Spanish word for "girl." Venezuelan girls and women are known throughout the world for their success in beauty pageants, or contests. The Miss Venezuela pageant is the most glamorous and competitive in all of South America. It is usually the most-watched TV event of the year.

FAST FACT:
No country in the world has had more international beauty pageant winners than Venezuela.

O is for oil.

Venezuela's economy depends largely on oil exports. When explorers discovered oil in Venezuela in 1914, Venezuela quickly became a much richer country. Today, Venezuela is one of the world's top oil producers.

FAST FACT:
Many of Venezuela's oil fields are near the Orinoco River, the country's largest river.

P is for piñata.

A piñata is a colorful cardboard and paper container filled with candy and other treats. At a birthday party, Venezuelan children often take turns swatting at a piñata hanging from the ceiling. When the piñata breaks, everyone scrambles to grab the goodies off the floor.

Q is for queso blanco
(KAY-soh BLAHN-koh).

Queso blanco is a white cheese similar to mozzarella and cottage cheese. Made by hand from fresh cow or goat milk, *queso blanco* is often stuffed inside flat breads or puffed pastries. Some Venezuelans, however, simply eat it plain.

FAST FACT:
Unlike many American cheeses, *queso blanco* does not melt when it is heated. It just becomes warm and soft.

R is for Roman Catholicism.

When Spanish missionaries came to Venezuela hundreds of years ago, they brought Roman Catholicism with them. Today, almost 95 percent of Venezuelans are Roman Catholic. Every village has at least one church.

FAST FACT:
Many Venezuelan villages have a special patron saint. Residents believe the saint protects them from harm.

S is for sports.

Baseball is the most popular sport in Venezuela. Many Venezuelan athletes go to the United States to play major league baseball. Basketball and soccer are also popular sports. Each year, Venezuela's national soccer team tries to qualify for the World Cup tournament.

T is for tepuis (teh-PWEES).

Tepuis are the large, flat-topped mountains along the Orinoco River region of Venezuela. One of these mountains is the site of Angel Falls, the highest waterfall on Earth. There, the Churun River drops 3,212 feet (974 meters). Angel Falls is in Canaima National Park.

FAST FACT:
Venezuela is also home to Lake Maracaibo, the largest lake in South America.

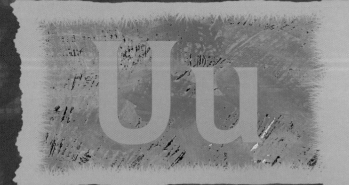

U is for unico (OO-nee-koh).

A word many Venezuelans use to describe their country is *unico*, or unique.

Few countries have such a wide range of landscapes, natural resources,

people, and wildlife—all rolled into one country.

V is for Valencia.

Valencia is Venezuela's fourth largest city and one of the country's industrial centers. Items produced there include cars, chemicals, and textiles. Since it is located in a farming area, Valencia is also a center for sugarcane, cotton, and cattle.

FAST FACT:
Valencia was founded in 1555. It was Venezuela's capital city for two short periods of time.

W is for Waraira Repano.

Waraira Repano is the local name for one of three beautiful mountains in Avila National Park. These mountains separate Caracas from the Caribbean Sea. Also called the Avila Mountain, Waraira Repano rises 6,500 feet (1,972 m) above sea level.

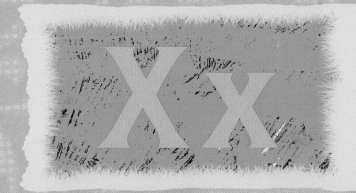

X is for exports.

Venezuela's largest export is oil. Other exports include coal, chemicals, aluminum, and steel. The country also exports several agricultural products, such as rice, tropical fruits, and coffee.

FAST FACT:
Venezuela exports most of its products to the United States, Mexico, Columbia, and Brazil.

Yy

Y is for
Yanomami.

The Yanomami are a native Venezuelan group. They live and work in the rain forest as their ancestors did for hundreds of years. They wear traditional clothing and sleep in houses made from leaves and other plant materials.

FAST FACT:
There are a number of other native Venezuelan groups, including the Guajira people. The Guajira live in northwestern Venezuela.

Z is for zapato
(zah-PAH-toh)

Zapato means "shoe." Venezuelans use leather and fabrics to make many kinds of shoes. Many rural people wear simple, comfortable shoes made of canvas. The soles of these shoes are made of rope.

Venezuela in Brief

Official name: Venezuela

Capital: Caracas

Official language: Spanish

Population: about 26 million

People: Spanish, Italian, Portuguese, Arab, German, African, indigenous people (including the Yanomami and the Guajira)

Religions: about 95 percent Roman Catholic, 2 percent Protestant, 3 percent other

Education: required from age 7 to 15

Major holidays: New Year's Day (January 1), Carnival (February/March), Palm Sunday (March/April), Easter (March/April), Labor Day (May 1), Independence Day (July 5), All Saints' Day (November 5), Christmas Day (December 25), New Year's Eve (December 31)

Transportation: cars, boats, airplanes

Climate: tropical; hot, humid; more moderate in the highlands

Total area: 364,820 square miles (912,050 square kilometers)

Highest point: Pico Bolivar (La Columna), 16,523 feet (5,007 meters)

Lowest point: Caribbean Sea, sea level

Type of government: republic

Most powerful government official: president

Major industries: oil, iron ore mining, construction materials, food processing, textiles, steel, aluminum

Major agricultural products: corn, sorghum, sugarcane, rice, bananas, vegetables, coffee, beef, pork, milk, eggs, fish

Chief exports: oil, coal, chemicals, aluminum, steel, agricultural products

National symbol: coat of arms

Money: bolivar

Say It in SPANISH

hello .... *hola* (OH-lah)

goodbye .... *adios* (ah-dee-OHS)

please .... *por favor* (POHR fah-VOHR)

thank you .... *gracias* (GRAH-see-ahs)

yes .... *sí* (SEE)

no .... *no* (NOH)

Glossary

ancestors—relatives who lived several generations ago

caiman—alligator-like reptiles

coat of arms—the official symbol of a country, family, state, or organization

congress—the branch, or part, of government that makes laws

economy—a country's trade in products, services, and money

equator—the imaginary line around Earth's middle; it divides the northern half from the southern half

lagoon—a shallow body of water usually connected to a larger one

manatee—a large animal that looks like a seal; also called a sea cow

maracas—musical rattles

missionaries—people who travel the world, bringing their religion to other people

provinces—geographic divisions within a country

qualify—to earn the right to play

Roman Catholicism—a Christian religion; Christians believe that Jesus was the son of God

To Learn More

At the Library

Aalgaard, Wendy. *Venezuela in Pictures*. Minneapolis: Lerner Publications, 2005.

Gibson, Karen. *Venezuela: A Question and Answer Book*. Mankato, Minn.: Capstone Press, 2007.

Ng, Yumi. *Welcome to Venezuela*. Milwaukee: Gareth Stevens Publishing, 2004.

Shields, Charles J. *Venezuela*. Philadelphia: Mason Crest Publishers, 2004.

On the Web

FactHound offers a safe, fun way to find Web sites related to this book. All of the sites on FactHound have been researched by our staff.

1. Visit *www.facthound.com*
2. Type in this special code: 140482250X
3. Click on the FETCH IT button.

Your trusty FactHound will fetch the best sites for you!

Index

Angel Falls, 23
animals, 7, 12
art, 4
beauty pageants, 17
Bolívar, Simón, 5
Caracas, 3, 6, 10, 26, 30
cheese, 20
El Dorado, 8
exports, 18, 27, 30
flag, 9
food, 11, 16, 20, 27, 30
fruits, 16, 27, 30
Gallegos, Rómulo, 10
language, 3, 30
llanos, 15

location, 3
metric system, 14
money, 5, 30
music, 13
oil, 8, 18, 27, 30
piñatas, 19
population, 3, 6, 30
Roman Catholicism, 21, 30
shoes, 29
Spain, 5, 9
sports, 22
Valencia, 25
Waraira Repano, 26
Yanomami, 28, 30

Look for all of the books in the Country ABCs series:

Australia ABCs
Brazil ABCs
Canada ABCs
China ABCs
Costa Rica ABCs
Egypt ABCs
France ABC
Germany ABCs
Guatemala ABCs
India ABCs

Israel ABCs
Italy ABCs
Japan ABCs
Kenya ABCs
Mexico ABCs
New Zealand ABCs
Russia ABCs
The United States ABCs
Venezuela ABCs
Vietnam ABCs